JUMP STARTS FOR CATECHISTS

The Liturgical Year

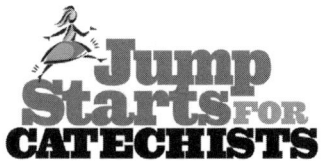

DAN CONNORS

The Liturgical Year

Twenty-Third Publications
A Division of Bayard
185 Willow Street
P.O. Box 180
Mystic, CT 06355
(860) 536-2611 or (800) 321-0411
www.twentythirdpublications.com
ISBN:1-58595-513-2

Copyright ©2005 Daniel Connors. All rights reserved. No part of this publication may be reproduced in any manner without prior written permission of the publisher. Write to the Permissions Editor.

Contents

About This Series	1
Introduction	3
1. How Our Liturgical Year Began	5
2. Advent	12
3. Christmas	20
4. Lent	24
5. The Sacred Triduum	29
6. Easter	36
7. Ordinary Time	39
8. Fast Facts about the Liturgical Year	43

About This Series

The *Jump Starts for Catechists* series offers catechists
 quick, hands-on tips for their faith formation sessions.
Each booklet provides practical and classroom-tested
 information, formation, and ideas
 that are valuable for beginning
  as well as experienced catechists.
The books are written by some of
 Twenty-Third Publications' best-selling authors,
  including Gwen Costello, Sr. Mary Kathleen Glavich,
   Daniel Connors, and Alison Berger.
Other books available in this series include
 Stories that Teach, *The Early Church*, and *The Prayer Journey*.

The Liturgical Year

Before catechists can teach the church seasons effectively,
 they need to be in touch with them themselves.
This highly readable, insightful resource
 speaks of the essential meaning of the seasons,
 where they came from, how we celebrate them,
  but most of all how they help us—catechists and learners—
  join our lives to the dying and rising of Jesus.
The Liturgical Year is ideal for busy catechists,
 as well as for any adult seeking a deeper understanding
  of the liturgical year.

Introduction

I remember the hopeful smile
   slowly fading from her face.
After a week of teaching kids in a Catholic school,
   Sister had given up another Saturday morning
   to teach us, the fifth graders
      in the St. Joseph religious ed program.
Once again, we were testing her faith.
Christmas was coming,
   and Sister Mary Anthony repeated her question.
"What are your families doing
   to get ready for the birth of our Lord?"
Again, no reply. We sat there and looked at her.
"Oh, come on, now," she said,
   "surely your families are doing
      more than thinking of presents!
   Who has an Advent wreath at home?" Silence.
She turned to me as if I were her last hope.
   "Danny, your family has an Advent wreath, don't they?"
      "Yes, Sister," I said.
The smile came back to her.
   "Yes," she said, "I knew your family would."
Then Sister, her faith in family life restored,
   went on to tell the class all about Advent wreaths.
To this day I remember my relief
   that she didn't ask me to tell about them,
      for, forgive me, Sister, but my answer was a lie.

We didn't have an Advent wreath at home.
    I didn't even know what an Advent wreath was.
Advent wreaths had escaped me completely.

Many of the persons you teach may be like I was then.
How can you help them get in touch
    with the seasons of the church year,
        seasons that have been developing for two thousand years
            in countless Catholic cultures,
            all mixing and blending together,
                always open to new experiences and new practices?

Before we can teach the seasons effectively,
    we need to be in touch with them ourselves.
I'd like to tell you some of the things
    I've learned about the seasons of the church's year
        since my fifth-grade encounter with Sister Mary Anthony.
In a small booklet there's no way
    to speak of all the seasonal practices
        of our very multicultural church.
Therefore I'll speak mostly
    of the essential meaning of the seasons,
    hoping you'll let my thoughts remind you
    of all the ways you and the persons you teach
    celebrate them—
        the customs you practice,
        and all the ways the church invites us
        through the seasons
        to gather and celebrate,
            and grow closer to our Lord.

Chapter 1

How Our Liturgical Year Began

Right now, the Catholic church in English-speaking countries
   is working on a new translation of the Roman Missal.
This large book contains all the prayers
   said at Mass throughout the year.
The church starts with the Roman Missal in Latin.
Then a group of translators gets to work,
   with input from the various national conferences of bishops
      in English-speaking countries
   and the appropriate sacred congregations in Rome.
After all the bishops' conferences finally approve the translation,
   it goes to Rome.
When everything is ready and approved,
   the new Roman Missal in English goes to the printer,
      and, "ta da!" Here it is!
That's the way things work
   in our very organized church these days.
However, the seasons of the church year
   didn't develop like that.

A Pope Sixtus or Clement didn't decide one day
    to have an Advent or a Lent or an Easter.
Nor was the matter turned over to a committee of bishops,
    who, after a few years of work,
        sent the newly minted church year
            back to the pope for approval.
No, the seasons of the church year developed
    a little at a time over centuries.
And it all began with Sunday.

Sunday

The earliest Christians
    celebrated one special day—Sunday—
        which appears under many names in Scripture
            and in the early church.
It was the "first day of the week,"
    when Christians would assemble
    to be with Jesus in the "breaking of the bread,"
    one of the very early names for what we know as the Mass.
Sunday was the glorious "day of resurrection,"
    the day on which Christ conquered sin and death
        and rose triumphant from the grave.
It was the "day of light" when, by rising from the grave,
    Christ broke the powers of darkness.
Sunday was the "day of the Spirit,"
    when Christ came and breathed the Spirit on the disciples.
It was known as the "eighth day":
    not just the start of a new week
        but the beginning of a new way of life,
        a new creation in Christ.
Sunday was our original holyday, our primary feast day.
It still is the heart of our year.

Tensions and Conflicts

Those first Christians who gathered on Sundays
    brought with them their own cultures and celebrations.
Jewish Christians continued to pray in Temple and synagogue
    and almost certainly celebrated
    the traditional Jewish feasts and seasons.
Gentile Christians probably still felt drawn
    to the festivals of the Roman world
        of which they were a part.
Over time, however, both Jewish and Gentile Christians
    would have felt an increasing tension
    between their new faith
        and the older beliefs and practices of their cultures.
What was compatible with their new faith?
    What was clearly incompatible?
    What could be re-imagined in a Christian form?

Liturgical Year "Stew"

All this may seem like ancient history,
    which, in one sense, it is.
But it's also the recipe and cooking pot
    out of which the seasons of our church year developed.
We start with the nourishing,
    substantial stock of faith in Christ;
        season it with varying amounts of the practices
        —and tension with the practices—
            that Christians brought from their cultures.
We continue to add these ingredients
    as the centuries pass and new cultures enter the church.
Include generous amounts of developing faith and theology,
    bring it all to a boil in conflict and persecution,
        and stir for a thousand years.

Slowly, something like the aroma
  of our liturgical year begins to rise.
Hold on a minute!
  I forgot something.
It happens a lot to me
  when I try my hand at cooking or baking.
A key ingredient is missing
  from the recipe I offered above.
Throw all those ingredients together
  and boil and stir for a thousand years
  and you still won't get Liturgical Year Stew.
The missing ingredient,
  the ingredient that pulls everything together
    and actually turns it into a liturgical year,
  is the need to welcome, form,
  and initiate new Christians into this new way of life
    through baptism, confirmation, and Eucharist.

The Key Ingredient

Welcoming and initiating new Christians
  seemed simple in the beginning.
Luke tells us that some 3000 persons
  were baptized on the day of Pentecost (Acts 2:41).
Philip met an Ethiopian on the road
  and instructed him about Jesus.
  The Ethiopian said, "Look, there is water.
    What is to prevent me from being baptized?" (Acts 8:36).
  Not a thing.
As the church grew
  and spread throughout the Roman empire, however,
    several things happened.

First, the church met resistance and sporadic persecutions,
    some of them quite severe.
Second, more and more new Christians
    came from cultures that were very different
        from the Jewish culture of the church's origins.
Third, from its humble beginnings,
    Christianity, with the Spirit's help, of course,
        became increasingly sophisticated.
Some first-rate thinkers and theologians
    wrote gospels and letters,
        and treatises reflecting on Christ, the church, and faith.
Fourth, almost from the very beginning,
    believing Christian groups developed different ideas
    about who Christ was, who God was,
        what salvation meant,
        and how Christians should live.
Out of the conflict among these groups,
    ideas of what was "orthodox"
    and what was "heretical"
        gradually developed.
Fifth, in the late fourth century,
    Christianity became the official religion of the empire.
The floodgates opened
    and the church was swamped
        with persons wanting to join.
In all these cases,
    the church faced fundamental questions—
    questions that had existed from the very beginning,
        but which became increasingly strong and focused.
    What does it mean to be a Christian?
    How does being a Christian affect our lives?
    How do we help newcomers understand
        the mystery of our salvation?

The church today calls this the "paschal mystery,"
   the redeeming life, death, and resurrection of Christ,
   his living in us today,
      and his coming again at the end of time.
How do we join our lives to this paschal mystery
   and share in Christ's redeeming life?
How do we live in Christ
   as individuals and as a community?
How do we help newcomers grow in Christ
   so that they can say with St. Paul,
      "I live now, not I, but Christ lives in me"?
This is the missing ingredient in the recipe above.
The need to offer good, solid formation
   to men and women who wanted to become Christians,
      helped spark the development of the liturgical seasons.
Eventually, mixed with all the other ingredients
      it gave us the liturgical year as we know it today.
This ingredient is also the best key for all of us
   as we think about and seek to live
      the seasons of the year in our own day.
The liturgical year is all about
   conversion and transformation.
The liturgical year is still the way
   we welcome and form new Christians.
The llturgical year is still an essential way
   for all of us to enter more deeply into our faith.
Year after year, the liturgical year teaches us
   how to live in God's time,
      to become aware of and to be part of
         the coming of the kingdom of God in our midst.
It teaches us to live in Christ's paschal mystery,
   remembered through the course
      of the whole liturgical year.

The Paschal Mystery

We go to Mass every Sunday
  through all the seasons of the year
    to give thanks and praise to God,
    to be nourished by the word of God
    and the body and blood of our Savior.
We go to be transformed more and more
  by the Holy Spirit into the Body of Christ.
We were baptized so that we may move ever more deeply
  into Christ's paschal mystery,
    learning to give of ourselves for others, as he did,
    and to die to our own selfish wants and desires
    by learning to live a life of generosity, forgiveness,
      justice, reconciliation, and healing.
Through the Mass and through the whole liturgical year,
  we join ourselves to Christ, dying with him
    so that we and the world may rise with him.
This pattern of dying and rising
  is meant to become the rhythm of our whole lives.
This paschal mystery, this rhythm of dying and rising,
  is what the church's liturgical year is really all about.
Without it, we've got Advent wreaths and Christmas holly,
  lenten diets and Easter butterflies.
By themselves these practices probably wouldn't have
  a lot of power to touch or transform our lives.

In the following chapters, we'll take a brief look
  at the seasons of the church year,
    where they come from, how we celebrate them,
    but most of all, how they help us join our lives
      to the dying and rising of Jesus.
Then, over our lifetime may we, too, say with St. Paul,
  "I live now, not I, but Christ lives in me."

Chapter 2

Advent

Several years ago,
   a family friend was working
      at the box office of Radio City Music Hall in New York City.
Around the first of August
   things started to get a little crazy there.
The lines at the ticket windows grew longer,
   customers started to sound frantic,
   and exhausted sales agents
      began to talk about "burnout."
The cause of all this excitement
   was not a Rolling Stones or Sinatra concert.
No, this was the mad rush to get tickets
   for the big Radio City Christmas Show,
      which ran that year from November 10 to January 3.
You're probably not surprised at that.
We all know what we're up against
   when it comes to celebrating the season of Advent.
Unless we've found a way to escape from the world entirely,
   Thanksgiving, at the latest,
      signals the beginning of a frenzied, often exhausting time.

No matter how hard we try
>   to celebrate the liturgical season of Advent
>   as it is meant to be,
>   the odds are against us.
Like the thousands of people
>   who wait in 90-degree August heat
>   to buy tickets for a Christmas show,
>   our culture calls us to live
>   with a confusion of calendars.
Like some of those ticket buyers,
>   we, too, may end up being just a little tired of Christmas
>   before the curtain even goes up.
Yet there are good reasons to hold on to Advent,
>   because of the way Advent developed
>   and what it really means today.

The Beginnings

Advent is a time of preparation for Christmas.
It may have begun as a short penitential time
>   or as a period of fasting
>   preparing for the great feast,
>   or of being ready for the second coming of Christ.
Some scholars also think that,
>   in some parts of the Eastern church,
>   the beginnings of Advent might have been
>   connected with preparing newcomers
>   for initiation at Epiphany.
Whatever its beginnings,
>   Advent evolved and spread throughout the church.
Our ancestors found Advent worth keeping,
>   and this season still holds a depth and beauty
>   that we shouldn't let our culture just wipe away.
Advent is more than a signal to get out the tree

and head for the mall.
It is more than looking forward to Christmas.
Advent is a liturgical season in its own right,
   and it says something very real and very important
      about who we are
         and how we share in the dying and rising of Jesus.
We can help one another
   discover and rediscover this liturgical season,
      so we can bring its message to the world.

A Time for Warmth and Light

For those of us in the colder areas
   of the northern hemisphere,
      Advent arrives with the deepening of winter,
         a time when our world is growing dark and bitter cold.
In less comfortable times,
   before central heating, for example,
      we drew closer together for survival in the cold.
Even today we like to gather
   around the warmth of a fire
      and light lamps to dispel the darkness.
We share stories that speak of hope in a barren world,
   and we wait.

Hope

Even if your winter climate
   allows for palm trees and beach outings,
      that word, hope, connects us all.
We live in a world
   that often seems cold and barren.
Wars, terrorism, crime, selfishness, injustice—
   sin in all its varieties is very much with us.
Just as we in cold winter areas

can lament the bone-chilling cold
and seemingly endless gray days,
 so all of us can raise a cry of lament to God.
Many of us feel deep inside
 a longing for *something*,
 something that will make us feel
 whole, complete.
No matter how wonderful
 our families, our jobs, and our parishes,
 we often feel a deep spiritual restlessness,
 an inner hunger that fails to be satisfied.
The Scripture and our church tradition see this
 as a deep inner longing to be one with God
 and in right relationship with one another.
We proclaim
 "Christ has died, Christ is risen!"
So why is our world such a mess,
 and so many of our lives incomplete?
All of creation is groaning, says St. Paul,
 for the redemption won in Christ to be completed.
This is why we put such hope
 in proclaiming that "Christ will come again,"
 when all will be made right,
 all will be complete,
 and every tear will be wiped away.
Hope. The church calls Advent
 a season of "joyful expectation."
It's a season of hope.
Sure, we prepare to remember and celebrate
 an event that happened some 2000 years ago—
 the birth of Jesus the Christ,
 the true hope and light of the world.
But at the same time, and with equal importance,

the first two weeks of Advent
> are devoted especially to waiting
>> for his second coming at the end of time,
>>> when justice shall triumph and all will be set right.

Standing between those two events of his coming
> and his coming again,
>> we look forward and backward
>>> so we can ask what God wants of us *now*.

We look forward and backward
> so that we can see the signs
>> of God's word and action in our lives *now*.

We hunger and long for the fulfillment
> of what Christ has started in us *now*.

We prepare to celebrate the birth of Christ,
> not just in Bethlehem,
>> but in our own lives *now*.

In this way we may share in his dying and rising
> and make that the rhythm of our own lives.

By doing so we help bring about the kingdom,
> here and now.

Already, but Not Yet

When my wife was pregnant
she spoke about knowing that the baby was with her,
> yet how she longed to hold him.

To celebrate Advent
> means to live with this kind of joyful expectation.

It also means coming to terms
> with ambiguity and tension.

It means having and not having all at the same time.

Think about it: we prepare for a birth
> that has already happened.

We celebrate a birth in us
> that has yet to be fulfilled.

We are a saved people
> living in the midst of our own sin,
> a risen people who still have to die,
> a people longing for a justice
>> that we have to help realize,
>>> even when it means dying a little,
>>> surrendering our will to God's.

We are citizens of heaven rooted on the earth,
> a people living in the glow of a light
>> still not fully revealed.

Being Christian/Advent people
> means to live with the tension
>> of being in two places at the same time.

We let the joyful tension
> between "longing" and "having" build
>> until it can be contained no more.

What Does this Mean for Us?

So how do we observe this season well?
Obviously we can't tell our kids or grandkids
> we won't go to their Christmas plays
> or tell our employers
>> that we won't go to the company party
>>> because these events are held in Advent.

But we can encourage our parishes
> to keep Advent well and to let it unfold
> without diluting both it and Christmas
>> by flowing one into the other too quickly.

We can keep Advent wreaths in our homes
> and think about all the ways
>> we and our world need Christ's ever increasing light.

We can sing Advent songs such as
    "People Look East" and "O Come Emmanuel"
        and other beautiful songs
            that speak of waiting in confident, joyful hope.
Outside of Sunday Mass we can sing them softly to ourselves
    as we drive or sort laundry or do any other small tasks.
We can spend time with Mary in prayer and song,
    and we can make her Magnificat (Luke 1:46–55)
        a part of our daily prayer.
With Mary's Magnificat to lead us,
    we can look around
    at all the ways Christ is calling us
        to die to ourselves and rise with him
            for the sake of the world,
                especially remembering the poor and the lowly.

We can hear Christmas carols
    and let the decorations and lights
    remind us of what we already have
        and still long for,
    what we are, and are becoming,
        the joy of living in, through, and with Christ.
As we shop for gifts we can remember
    that all the gifts we buy and give
    are signs and imitations of the great gift-giver,
    God,
        who gives us our world, our life,
        the Redeemer,
        the Spirit, grace, eternal life.
To give gifts out of love,
    especially to those in need,
        is to share a little in the very life of God.
Dying and rising is never neat.

In our lives it's never just one
> followed directly by the other.

Outside we may rush for presents,
> and share the early Christmas of the world.

But as we go about our daily lives,
> we can remember that what we have we still long for.

What we celebrate is still waiting
> to be fully revealed.

By remembering this,
> we may build an energy and a longing
>> and create a joy that can carry us
>>> past December 25 into the whole Christmas season.

Such joy can warm us until what we hope for
> finally comes to pass.

Chapter 3

Christmas

"You're a mean one, Mister Grinch."
   I've often been called a Grinch.
Who but a Grinch would ask people
   to look beyond the lights and evergreens
      and holly wreaths and the sweet baby in the manger?
No, it just doesn't feel like Christmas without these things.
Okay, leave them all as a sign of the coming kingdom,
   like the heavenly banquet hall Jesus so often talked about.
But in the midst of it all,
   the church's liturgical season of Christmas
      calls us to something deeper.
It calls us to celebrate the Christmas
   we've been preparing for throughout all of Advent.
Advent began with ominous readings
   about the end of the world
      and the second coming of Christ.
John the Baptizer called all of us
   to change our ways because the Savior is coming.
Advent reminded us of the prophets' hope for a Messiah
   bringing justice and peace.

We recalled Mary and Joseph,
> a young, unmarried, pregnant couple,
>> surrendering themselves to the will of God.

With all the wreaths and lights and sentiment,
> Christmas is the same paschal mystery,
>> the dying and rising that leads to *Life*.

About fifteen years ago, the bishops of the United States
> were developing a Scripture translation
>> for Masses with children.

I remember reading that some of the bishops
> weren't pleased with the way
> certain words were translated.

The traditional word "manger," for example,
> was being translated for the children
>> as a "feed box" for animals.

Sure, "manger" seems more poetic than "feed box."
Yet how many children, or adults, understand
> that a manger is indeed a feeding trough?

Jesus was laid in a feed box
Even then he was the paschal lamb,
> food for a hungry, starving world.

The Beginning of Christmas

The beginnings of the Christmas season
> had much less to do with a newborn baby—
>> and probably even less to do with the baby's birthday—
> than with the reason that baby was born:
>> salvation and life in the kingdom of God.

In fact, Christmas came late to the liturgical calendar.
The elder feast of what is now the Christmas season
> was Epiphany.

Epiphany may have started as a celebration
> of the baptism of Jesus.

It may have served, for a time and for some places,
    as a moment to welcome newcomers into the church
    by their dying and rising
        through the sacraments of initiation.
It was a paschal celebration.
The Jewish people do not seem to have made much fuss
    over celebrating birthdays.
That was more a custom
    of the pagan peoples of the empire.
As these peoples became Christian,
    they might have wanted to celebrate Jesus' birthday,
        but no one knew the date of his birth.
In our own time, around December 25th,
    newspapers carry stories
    about how Christians chose December 25
        in order to replace a pagan festival of the sun.
But scholars aren't so sure.
For we also know that
    while some Christians may have worried
        about a pagan festival,
    others were seeing January 6
        as a day of Jesus' baptism.
They often connected his birth, baptism, and death,
    seeing them as happening
        on the same day of the year.
Some thought Good Friday happened on April 6.
    Others thought the date was March 25.
So these Christians also considered these days
    to be the dates of his birth and baptism.
Christmas? on March 25? April 6?
    Maybe, for some of these early Christian thinkers.
But wait, someone said,
    his annunciation and conception are what count.

Jesus would have been conceived
> on the same day he died: March 25 or April 6.
So they set the date of the annunciation,
> and then counted forward nine months,
>> to December 25 (or January 6: Epiphany!)
Let the scholars wrangle over the details.
The point is, from the very beginning,
> Christmas has been strongly connected
>> to Jesus' death and resurrection.
The moment he took on our humanity
> his death became part of his life.
His resurrection was the vindication
> of a God who loved us enough to become one of us
>> and to invite us to share his life.
This is what Christmas celebrates—
> God's glorious gift of salvation.
That gift is celebrated and remembered in various ways
> through the whole Christmas season,
>> from Christmas Eve, through Epiphany,
>> to the feast of the Baptism of the Lord.

During this whole season we can
> keep our trees bright with joy,
> perhaps holding back a few gifts to share
>> on the other feasts and Sundays of Christmas,
> and getting involved in justice or service projects.
This is a whole season to keep, and in keeping it well
> to marvel at—and gradually come to share more deeply—
>> the glorious gift of God's love,
>>> a love strong enough to lead us through death
>>>> to the fullness of life itself.

Chapter 4

Lent

Ashes and palms,
   wooden clappers and shrouded statues,
   mite boxes and giving things up—
for all of us, of whatever age,
   Lent is a season of memories and power.
Lent resonates deep in our Catholic souls.

How Should We Celebrate?

More and more, however,
   Lent also seems to be a time of some confusion.
   Should we concentrate on our sins?
   Should we still give things up?
   Is fasting still meaningful in our modern world?
   Or would our Lent be better spent working
      in the local soup kitchen
      or writing to Congress about justice issues?
Perhaps it would be wise
   to begin by looking briefly at the origins of the season
      and remembering a few of the reasons
         why we have Lent in the first place.

It is impossible to pinpoint
exactly when or how Lent started.
The further scholars look into the question,
   the more complicated it becomes.
Different traditions of fasting,
   different lengths of time,
      different approaches to the season,
         different beginning and ending times—
   wherever we look in the early church
   we see a multilayered story
      and a variety of practices
         that only gradually began to connect and blend
         into the Lent we know today.
When the observance of Lent was finally more established,
   its heart was centered firmly on baptism.
Over the centuries
   the Easter Vigil had become the time
      when new life was welcomed
      into the Christian community
         through baptism, confirmation, and Eucharist.
In many parts of the church
   adult catechumens spent years
      learning to live the life of the community,
         the life Christ lived.
When they and the community
   felt they were ready for the sacraments of initiation,
   these catechumens would become the Elect—
   those who were chosen to be baptized—
      and they began intense preparations for the Vigil.
This preparation time was thought ideally to last forty days,
   symbolizing, among other things,
      the time Christ spent in the desert
         and the forty years the Jews wandered in the wilderness.

During this time the Elect fasted and prayed,
   and the community fasted and prayed with them,
      both to show their support for the Elect
      and to prepare to renew
         their own baptismal commitment at the Vigil.
At about the same time,
   people who had sinned grievously
   were in the process of being welcomed back
      into the community through an order of penitents,
         with some similarities to the catechumenate.
So the lenten season also took on a penitential tone.
During Lent, the community and the Elect
   prayed that they might hear the word of God
      and be open to God's Spirit.
They fasted as a spiritual discipline,
   as a way of making room
   in their hearts for the Spirit,
Fasting reminded them that, before anything else,
   even before their need for food,
   they were utterly dependent
      on "every word that comes from the mouth of God."
They made a special effort to practice charity
   because their openness to the Spirit
   and their realization of their dependence on God
      would lead them to live the life Christ lived,
         a life for others.
Prayer, fasting, and almsgiving:
   this was the path to the waters of life and death.
This was how the community prepared
   to renew its baptismal life
      and be joined, ever more intensely,
         to the dying and rising of Christ.

Lent Today

What was true then is still true today.
Baptism is still the heart of Lent,
    and sharing in the dying and rising of Christ
        is still the heart of baptism.
This is true of all the sacraments, of course,
    especially the Eucharist we celebrate and receive every week.
Whatever lenten practices we choose,
    the best will always be those solidly rooted in baptism.
So we need to come to terms
    with what baptism is all about.
A Lent rooted in baptism
    means coming face to face with life and death,
    with crucifixion and resurrection,
We learn what it means and what it costs
    to put aside the old self
    and let Christ live in us,
        to be part of Christ's community,
            and to share in his Spirit.
A Lent rooted in baptism means praying
    that we may be open to God's Spirit.
It means undertaking fasting and other disciplines,
    not as ends in themselves,
        but so we can clear away the clutter of our lives
            and see what is really important.
A Lent rooted in baptism means
    reaching out to help others,
    not because Lent is a time for charity,
        but because that is what following Christ is all about.
Lent means going into our spiritual deserts,
    not to hide from the world
    but to come face to face
        with the power of sin and death inside us.

We respond, as Jesus taught us
   by relying on the love, power, and mercy of God.
Lent means doing penance,
   not just in the sense
      of expressing sorrow or paying a penalty,
         but in the original gospel meaning of repentance,
            being so open to God that God changes our lives.
We have many ways to pray,
   many ways to fast,
      and many ways to give alms during Lent.
Whether the ways we choose
   are successful or not
      may depend on how well they lead us back to the font,
      how deeply they draw us
         into Christ's paschal mystery.
Their effectiveness depends on how well they help us
   be the new people our baptism calls us to be,
      not just for forty days but forever.

Chapter 5

The Sacred Triduum

The Sacred Triduum,
    the Three Holy Days,
        sit at the very center of our liturgical year.
They are the hub of the wheel
    of every disciple's life.
Everything we do and celebrate as disciples—
    the sacraments, our work, our families, our lives—
        is meant to draw us more deeply
            into living the paschal mystery,
                the saving, redeeming life of Christ
                that we bring to the world.
The Sacred Triduum, these Three Holy Days,
    bring it all into focus.

Three Days?

The Triduum starts late Thursday afternoon, as Lent ends,
    and it concludes with Evening Prayer
        on Easter Sunday evening.
Thursday, Friday, Saturday, Sunday?
    Three days, or four?

In liturgical time,
> the church follows the ancient Jewish practice
>> of a day starting in the evening.

So Thursday evening to Friday evening
> is the first day.

Friday to Saturday evening is the second day.

Saturday to Sunday evening is the third day.

To add to the confusion,
> the three principal celebrations of the Triduum,
>> the Thursday evening Mass of the Lord's Supper,
>> the Good Friday liturgy,
>> and the great Easter Vigil,
> are all considered one liturgy,
>> lived out over three days.

The Heart of the Triduum

The Triduum is very different from Lent.

In the Scriptures and liturgies of Lent,
> Jesus challenges us
>> to take a courageous look at God
>> and at ourselves.

He asks us to believe in a God
> who forgives and loves
> without counting the cost.

He asks us to believe
> that he carries God's life within him,
>> and that we can too.

By believing in him
> and joining our lives to his,
>> we can live more and more in his paschal mystery,
>>> the dying to self that brings life.

Now in the Triduum,
> it's time to embrace and *live* that life.

We'll remember and celebrate
    Jesus' supper with his friends,
        his passion and death, his rising to new life.
But this isn't costume-drama remembering.
It's not that "we are there,"
    it's that Christ is here.
The power of his one sacrifice
    is still saving, still redeeming
        through his Spirit.
We join our lives to his
    so that we may have the power
    to live his paschal mystery
        in all the events of our days.

In the gospel for Wednesday of Holy Week,
    the disciples ask Jesus:
        "Where do you wish us to prepare the passover supper?"
We have been preparing for this Triduum
    during Lent and for all of our lives.
The Elect, who will be initiated
    through baptism, confirmation, and Eucharist,
        have been preparing for this Triduum
            during Lent and all of their lives, too.
Together with them, *we* are the place
    where the passover meal is being prepared.
This Triduum is the door to life.
And the door to life is open.

Mass of the Lord's Supper

The gospels of Matthew, Mark, and Luke,
    all present the gift of the Eucharist
        in the context of Jesus' passion and death.
Giving and receiving Eucharist

has everything to do with the paschal mystery:
> the kind of dying that leads to life.

Perhaps to make sure we haven't missed the point,
> John's gospel tells us that
>> Jesus washed the feet of his disciples at the Last Supper.

Jesus asked them,
> "Do you realize what I have done for you?"

Do we realize what he has done for us?

He comes as a servant
> to shake up our ideas of God
>> and show us what God's love is really all about.

By his life, death, and resurrection,
> Jesus shows us that a life lived for others
>> is the only kind of life worth living.

He breaks down the barriers that we put up
> to keep us separated from one another.

He challenges us to live his life
> by sharing in the Eucharist
>> and being ready to wash one another's feet
>>> in any way life calls us to.

This is part of the dying and rising in Christ
> that our baptism calls us to share.

It is part of the commitment we make
> every time we receive the Eucharist.

When we receive Eucharist,
> we're taking our lives as they are now
>> and saying yes to our baptism,
>> yes to the community,
>> yes to justice and reconciliation,
>> yes to living Jesus' life in our own.

We who receive the Eucharist
> become the Eucharist,
>> sharing Christ's life by being food given for all.

Good Friday

This day is the only one in the whole church year
    when no Eucharist is celebrated.
But it is not a day of sorrow;
    it is a day of sober, serious joy.
The question Jesus asked us yesterday
    still echoes through the ages
        and in our lives:
    "Do you realize what I have done for you?"
Because of Jesus, and what Jesus willingly gave up,
    faith shows us a world of holiness and redemption
        where sinners can be forgiven,
        wounds can be healed,
        hopes can be fulfilled,
        and the dead can be raised to life.
Because of what Jesus did on this day,
    we now have a great High Priest
        offering an eternal liturgy
        of thanks and praise to God
            and interceding for the life of the world.
Our baptism gives us a share
    in Christ's life and worship.
When we worship,
    we're joining Christ in his liturgy
        of praise and intercession.
In Christ we offer that worship
    every moment of our lives,
        in all our words and deeds.
Today when we remember what Christ has done,
    let's also remember
        who we are, because of what he has done.
For that we offer our thanks and praise!

The Easter Vigil

The great new fire is lit,
   and from it the paschal candle.
From that great candle are lit
   the candles of all the people,
      assembled to encounter and welcome
         new life and resurrection.
This night the people of God, the body of Christ,
   stand with lighted candles,
      each face illuminated, each light separate.
Yet each light comes
   from the one light of the risen Christ.
This is the great Christian assembly
   of neighbors, friends, strangers,
      all with separate stories,
      all with their own hopes and fears, sorrows and joys,
All of them share in the light of Christ.
This is the one body of Christ,
   the communion of saints
      spanning heaven and earth.
Heaven *is wedded* to earth,
   the Easter exultation proclaims,
      for on this night we remember how Christ
         broke the chains of death
         and rose triumphant from the grave.
Think of all the sorrows of our lives,
   all the ways we bind ourselves
      and are bound by others,
      by human history, and by society
         in a tomb of sin, selfishness, fear, and death.
Then listen to the readings and hear the story
   about God reaching out to us
      with the power to heal and to save.

This night the church,
    the body of Christ,
        joins itself to the Elect
            who will be baptized this night.
As the waters of rebirth wash over them,
    we have an opportunity
        to remember that these waters
        have also washed over us.
As the fragrance of the oils fills the church,
    we remember that the same anointing
        has been given to us.
As the newly baptized approach the banquet,
    we join them with joy,
        for through the Spirit's power,
            we are fed on Christ's body and blood
            and become his body and blood for others.
We are part of Christ,
    called to share his life in our own,
        so that the world may see and come to believe
            that God's love is real,
        and that all are invited to the banquet
            in God's kingdom of life and light.

This is the heart of the Triduum.
This is the heart of the liturgical year.
This is the heart of our lives as Catholic disciples.

Chapter 6

Easter

The paschal candle burns brightly.
The neophytes, those fully initiated at the Vigil,
   have received their white garments.
We have solemnly renewed our own baptismal promises:
   We believe in God…
   We believe in Jesus Christ…
   We believe in the Holy Spirit…
We have come forward together
   to share in the heavenly banquet of the Lamb.
The heavenly banquet,
   the victory of life over death, love over hatred,
   reconciliation over division.
How could one day contain such a celebration?
That is why, from as early as the third century,
   Christians have dedicated a full fifty days to the Easter season,
      from Easter Vigil to Pentecost.
Our ancestors found great meaning in these fifty days.
   Fifty days was a symbol of eternity.
   Fifty days is seven weeks,
      a week of weeks plus one day.

This was the eighth day,
> the same name they gave to the day of resurrection,
> the same name they used for Sunday,
>> the first day of the week.

For the early Christians and for us,
> this eighth day is not just the start
>> of a new seven-day week,
>>> but the beginning of a whole new creation,
>>> the beginning of life in the Spirit,
>>> the beginning of the "last days,"
>>> the celebration of living in Christ.

Fifty days is also just about one-seventh of the year,
> so these fifty days hold the same relation to the year
>> as Sunday does to the week.

That's why the fifty days of Easter
> are also known as the year's Great Sunday.

During this time we rejoice with the neophytes.
Together, we savor and ponder and grow
> into the saving mysteries we have experienced.

We welcome them into our communion,
> and we are re-inspired and renewed
>> by the freshness of their faith.

Easter is not a history lesson.
Only part of it is about what happened to Jesus
> some 2000 years ago.

Easter is also about what happens to us, *now*,
> because of Jesus.

Easter celebrates how Jesus
> dies and rises in us here and now,
>> in our parish,
>> in our classroom,
>> in our job and family,
>> in all the joys and sorrows of this world.

Easter is about how we and the world are changed
because of Jesus.

Mystagogia

The church calls this time Mystagogia,
   which is a Greek word for "savoring the mysteries."
In our Easter liturgies we and the neophytes
   are meant to hear and experience
   what it means when we say Christ is risen.
We hear and experience the first preaching of the apostles.
We ponder the beginnings of our church,
   the body of Christ,
   the meaning of discipleship,
      and life in the church together
         as we all follow the Good Shepherd.
We savor and ponder the gift of the Holy Spirit.
And, especially near the end
   of this Great Sunday,
   we reflect on our mission,
      on what joining in Eucharist
         commits us to be and to do.
For as glorious as the taste of the heavenly banquet
   is meant to be,
   a taste we renew at every Eucharist,
      we cannot spend all our time
         looking up into the sky.
Christ will return,
   and, like the disciples on Pentecost,
      we have dying and rising to do,
      and a mission to get under way.

Chapter 7

Ordinary Time

The word "Ordinary" in Ordinary Time
    doesn't mean ordinary in the usual sense.
Remember "ordinal" numbers—first, second, third?
That's what "ordinary" refers to here:
    the numbered Sundays of the year
        outside of the special seasons.
Yet Ordinary Time does seem rather ordinary.
    It doesn't bring any strong images to mind
        the way the other seasons do.
In fact, the Sundays of Ordinary Time
    don't all fall during the same time of the year.
To understand Ordinary Time,
    we need to understand the church year as a whole.
We need to remember the essential meaning
    of all the other seasons
        and then think about the rhythms of time.

The Rhythms of Time

The world our senses perceive is a rhythmic world.
The earth travels around the sun,

the moon travels around the earth…
   our world pulses in regular, discernible patterns.
Our human lives, too, thrive on patterns:
   the sound of the alarm clock and the late news,
      the clack of the commuter train
         taking us to work or bringing us home.
Researchers tell us we function better
   when we go to bed at a regular time
   and get up at a regular time.
We count the days until Christmas,
   welcome summer on Memorial Day,
   and bid it farewell on Labor Day.
Like breathing in and breathing out,
   rhythms and patterns mark our days,
      bringing order and coherence out of chaos.
Like breath itself, they bring life to our lives.
From Sunday Mass
   to daily morning and evening prayer,
      the same is true of our lives as Christians.
Our worship and our liturgical year
   have regular ritual patterns and rhythms.
That's what makes them ours
   and helps them give us life.

The Time Between

Ordinary Time is part of this rhythm.
It completes the pattern, the breath of the other seasons.
Ordinary Time developed not so much for what it is,
   but for what it is not.
It is not Easter, Lent, Advent, or Christmas.
Ordinary Time is not a special time of the year,
   but that makes it important in a different way.
Perhaps we can think of it this way.

Rhythms need at least two points:
    on-off, up-down, tension-release.
We can't just inhale; we also have to exhale.
Musical notes need silent spaces between them;
    silence is as much a part of music as sound is.
Would we really want to celebrate
    our birthday every day?
        After a while, what would make it special?
In the same way, without Ordinary Time
    would Advent, Christmas, Lent, the Triduum, and Easter
        still shine as brightly?

Entering the Season

Calling Ordinary Time a quiet time or an off time
    doesn't mean that it is unimportant!
Sunday, the primary element of the liturgical year,
    still marks our weeks.
Special solemnities and feasts are celebrated
    during this season.
Rather than focusing on distinctive aspects
    of the paschal mystery, as Lent, the Triduum,
        Easter, Advent, and Christmas do,
    Ordinary Time gives us an opportunity to ponder
        all the aspects of this mystery,
            as they unfold Sunday by Sunday.
In the gospels for the Sundays of Ordinary Time
    we follow Jesus through his public ministry,
        on his journey toward Jerusalem,
            to his death and resurrection.
It is our opportunity to journey with Jesus
    as he proclaims and reveals
        through word and deed,
            the paschal mystery and the kingdom of God.

We should have a special feeling for Ordinary Time,
  because most of our lives are spent
    doing very ordinary things:
      working, eating, paying bills, worrying, shopping, driving.
These are not very exciting, but they make up
  the rhythms of our lives much more
    than do birthdays and special occasions.
We are called to listen to God's voice,
  not just during the special seasons of the year,
    but always.
We are to carry out our Christian mission,
  not just on the holy days,
    but always.
We are to help the poor and work for justice,
  not just at Thanksgiving and Christmas,
    but always.
Ordinary Time is an opportunity
  to be the body of Christ in the midst of everyday life.
It is an opportunity to experience
  how God calls us to holiness
    in our daily rhythm of waking and resting,
      working and playing, laughing and worrying.
When we can find God here,
  how much more glorious
    the great seasons of our year will be!

Chapter 8

Fast Facts about the Liturgical Year

Several church documents speak about the liturgical year.
The General Norms for the Liturgical Year and the Calendar
    gives an outline of the year
    and the general scope of the seasons.
The General Instruction of the Roman Missal
    and the *Lectionary for Mass: Introduction*
    also give important information.
The liturgical year is very complex,
    difficult to describe accurately and briefly.
Please take what follows as general information.
There are numerous exceptions and nuances.

Subdivisions of the Year

The liturgical year
    is divided into two main parts
        that unfold simultaneously on their own schedules.
The temporal cycle includes the seasons of the church year,
    which we've been discussing in this book.

It also includes special solemnities and feasts,
 such as the solemnities of the Ascension,
  the Holy Trinity, and the Body and Blood of the Lord.
The sanctoral cycle is made up of the feasts of the saints,
 celebrated on a certain day each year.
As we have noted,
 Sunday is the main building block of the liturgical year.
Only certain solemnities of the Lord,
 such as those mentioned above,
  can replace a Sunday Mass.
Even then, they cannot replace the Sunday celebration
 during Advent, Lent, or Easter.

Catholics are used to speaking of feast days.
 But again, things are not so simple.
There are three levels
 of what are commonly known as feasts.
The most important feasts are called *solemnities*.
These days are considered equal to,
 and sometimes more important than, Sundays.
Some solemnities are holydays of obligation.
 These include the Immaculate Conception (December 8),
  Christmas (December 25)
  Mary, Mother of God (January 1),
  Ascension (now moved to Sunday in most U.S. dioceses),
  Assumption of the Blessed Virgin Mary (August 15),
  and All Saints Day (November 1).
Local churches might also celebrate as a solemnity
 their patron saint's day
  or the day commemorating
   the dedication of their church.
The next level of what are commonly known as feasts
 are actually called *feasts*.

These, typically, are feasts of Mary
   (such as her birth, September 8),
   feasts of apostles
      (such as the Conversion of Paul, January 25),
   or feasts of the Lord
      such as his Transfiguration (August 6).
After solemnities and feasts, the church celebrates *memorials*.
   These are days remembering certain saints.
To add to the complexity,
   memorials are divided into two groups:
   obligatory memorials,
      celebrations of saints important to the universal church,
      (Saint Francis on October 4, for example),
   and optional memorials,
      celebrations of saints who are most important
         to local churches.
Obligatory memorials have their own prayers.
Optional memorials are just that: optional.
If the presiding priest chooses to celebrate
   an optional memorial,
      he has several prayers from which to choose.

How do we know what is being celebrated on a particular day?
The universal church has a general liturgical calendar
   that gives rules, guidelines, and a general outline.
The bishops of the United States issue a general calendar
   based on the universal calendar, but adapted to the U.S.
Each diocese takes this calendar
   and can issue its own *ordo*,
      which is basically a liturgical calendar
      specifying which solemnity, feast, or memorial
         is to be celebrated each day in that diocese.

The Roman Missal

The Roman Missal is the church book
  containing all the prayers and readings
    of the eucharistic liturgy throughout the year.
This Missal is commonly divided into two parts or volumes:
  the *Sacramentary* and the *Lectionary*.
The *Sacramentary* contains the prayers of the Mass.
These prayers basically have two parts:
  the Ordinary and the Proper of the Mass.
The *Ordinary* of the Mass
  are those prayers that can be said at every Eucharist.
The opening greeting, the eucharistic prayers,
  and the Lamb of God, for example,
    are part of every Mass.
The *Proper* prayers are those prayers
  proper to a specific day.
Each Sunday has its opening prayers, for example,
  its own prayer over the gifts,
    and prayer after communion.
These are listed in the *Sacramentary* by the day.
The weekdays of Advent, Christmas, Lent, and Easter
  also have their own Proper prayers.
The weekdays of Ordinary time do not
  (the presider chooses from among
    the Proper prayers of the Sundays of Ordinary Time).
Solemnities, feasts, and obligatory memorials
  also have their own proper prayers.
For optional memorials, the presider
  can choose from among several prayers
    grouped together and found, for example,
      in the "common [prayers] of pastors,"
        "common of martyrs," "common of virgins."

The *Lectionary* has a complexity all its own.
There are readings for Sundays,
  solemnities, feasts, and memorials.
There are three readings on Sundays,
  which follow a three-year cycle,
    known as years A, B, and C.
In year A, the gospel readings
  are generally taken from Matthew.
  In year B, from Mark,
    and in year C, from Luke.
Usually (the Easter season being a major exception)
  the first reading is taken from the Old Testament,
  and is chosen for some thematic connection to the gospel.
The second reading
  is usually chosen from the New Testament letters
    and follows its own pattern.
Except during Advent and Lent
  it usually has no direct connection
  to the first reading or gospel.

The weekday readings mainly follow a two-year cycle.
  There are usually two readings on weekdays.
During Advent, Christmas, Lent, and Easter,
  the same weekday readings are used every year.
In Ordinary Time,
  the gospel is usually the same every year,
  and the first reading is taken from
    selected books of the Old and New Testament.
These are read through in a semi-continuous manner
  and alternate on a year I, year II cycle.
Solemnities have three readings;
  feasts and memorials have two.

The Seasons

Advent begins with the Sunday closest to November 30.
The liturgical color (vestments, etc.) is violet,
   usually a royal purple, a blue-purple.
      (The color blue is not officially approved.)
The Christmas season starts
   with evening prayer on December 24
      and continues until the Sunday after Epiphany
         (usually the Baptism of the Lord).
Christmas, like Easter, has an Octave,
   eight days of special importance and solemnity,
      which runs from Christmas day to January 1.
The liturgical colors are white and gold.

Lent begins on Ash Wednesday
   and ends before the evening Mass on Holy Thursday.
On the Third, Fourth, and Fifth Sundays of Lent
   the church celebrates the rites of scrutiny with the Elect.
These rites are meant to help raise up
   whatever is weak and sinful in the Elect
   (and in the community)
      and to fill them (and us) with the power of Christ,
      who can save us from sin and from death.
The scrutiny rites are rooted in the year A readings
   for those Sundays.
They include the gospels of the woman at the well,
   the man born blind,
      and the raising of Lazarus,
         all from the Gospel of John.
The liturgical color of Lent is violet,
   a reddish purple, the color of penance,
      with red being the color of martyrdom.

The *Triduum* is at the center of the liturgical year.
On Good Friday and Holy Saturday until the Vigil
>   the church calls for an Easter fast.
This is not a lenten penitential fast,
>   but more a fast of anticipation,
>>   preparing for the great celebration
>>>   of the resurrection.
Like Christmas, Easter has an octave;
>   each of the eight days is a solemnity of the Lord,
>>   concluding with the Second Sunday of Easter.
The Easter Season begins with the Easter Vigil
>   and ends fifty days later with Pentecost.
The liturgical color is white.

Ordinary Time is divided into two parts.
The short stretch runs
>   from Monday of the week after January 6,
>>   to the Tuesday before Ash Wednesday.
The much longer stretch extends from
>   the Monday after Pentecost
>>   until the Saturday before the first Sunday of Advent.
The feast of the Baptism of the Lord
>   replaces the First Sunday of Ordinary Time.
The solemnities of the Holy Trinity
>   and the Body and Blood of Christ
>>   replace two additional Sundays of Ordinary Time.
However, the weekdays after these Sundays
>   *are* part of Ordinary Time.
Ordinary Time's liturgical color is green.

The Liturgy of the Hours

No discussion of the liturgical year would be complete
>   without at least a mention of the Liturgy of the Hours.

The Liturgy of the Hours is
   the usual daily prayer of the church.
It follows the seasons and sanctoral feasts
   with its own daily times of prayers and readings,
      especially morning and evening prayer.
The Liturgy of the Hours invites us to begin our days
   with prayers of praise,
   and in the evening
      to express our thanksgiving for the day,
      and our sorrow for any wrong we may have done.
Through these liturgical moments of daily prayer,
   we join with the whole church
      to remember our dependence on God
      and rededicate ourselves to living in Christ.
In this way the Liturgy of the Hours
   is an important part
      of the daily, weekly, and seasonal cycle
      that connects us to the paschal mystery.
It is this mystery that we celebrate and live
      throughout the whole
         of our church's liturgical year.